KFK KINGFISHER KNOWLEDGE

ROCKS & FOSSILS

► Wavy layers of sandstone
form the Vermillion Cliffs
of Arizona.

KFK KINGFISHER KNOWLEDGE

ROCKS & FOSSILS

Margaret Hynes

Foreword by
Professor Jack Horner

KINGFISHER

BOSTON

Editor: Clive Wilson
Coordinating editor: Stephanie Pliakas
Senior designer: Peter Clayman
Consultant: Chris Pellant
Picture research manager: Cee Weston-Baker
Senior production controller: Lindsey Scott
DTP coordinator: Catherine Hibbert
DTP operator: Claire Cessford
Artwork archivist: Wendy Allison
Proofreaders: Sheila Clewley, Sarah Snavely

KINGFISHER

a Houghton Mifflin Company imprint
222 Berkeley Street
Boston, Massachusetts 02116
www.houghtonmifflinbooks.com

First published in 2006
10 9 8 7 6 5 4 3 2 1
1TR/0206/TWP/MA(MA)/130ENSOMA/F

Copyright © Kingfisher Publications Plc 2006

All rights reserved under International and
Pan-American Copyright Conventions

LIBRARY OF CONGRESS CATALOGING-IN-PUBLICATION DATA
has been applied for.

ISBN 0-7534-5974-4
ISBN 978-07534-5974-4

Printed in Singapore

GO FURTHER . . .
INFORMATION PANEL KEY:

web sites and
further reading

career paths

places to visit

NOTE TO READERS
The web site addresses listed in this book are
correct at the time of going to print. However, due to
the ever-changing nature of the Internet, web site
addresses and content can change. Web sites can
contain links that are unsuitable for children. The
publisher cannot be held responsible for changes
in web site addresses or content or for information
obtained through third-party web sites. We
strongly advise that Internet searches should be
supervised by an adult.

Contents

▲ Thousands of limestone pillars rise up out of the yellow sands of the Pinnacles desert in Western Australia. Some of these peculiar rock formations reach a height of 16 ft. (5m).

Foreword

When I was a young boy growing up in northern Montana, I had a tremendous curiosity and interest in learning about the past—not an interest in the human history of Montana or the United States but rather the prehistoric, ancient history of our entire planet. I wanted to know what the world was like millions—and even billions—of years ago. So, as a child and later as a young adult, I collected rocks and fossils and tried to figure out what kind of stories they told about the land where I lived. I even had my mother drive me to places like Alberta, Canada, where I'd heard that dinosaurs had been found. I started a rock and fossil collection, and I cataloged it so that I wouldn't forget where each piece had come from. While I was in high school I used my collection to create science projects, and before leaving my hometown for college, I donated much of my collection to the local museum. Now, some 40 years later, people visiting the Toole County Museum in Shelby, Montana, can still see my little collection of rocks and fossils that I put together when I was a young boy.

As I grew older and went to college, my interest in rocks and fossils became even stronger. In college I studied geology and biology and learned how and where to find particular rocks and fossils. At first, I studied 300-million-year-old rocks that contained fossil fish, shrimps, and brachiopods. Later, while I was still at college, I began a serious study of the rocks and fossils from the age of dinosaurs. I had become a dinosaur paleontologist.

At Princeton University I studied some of the first dinosaur fossils found in North America. These fossils were housed in one of the oldest natural history museums in the U.S., the Philadelphia Academy of Science. Interestingly for me, most of the dinosaur fossils in their collections had come from my home state of Montana. I soon moved back to Montana to work at the Museum of the Rockies in Bozeman, where I began building one of the world's largest dinosaur research programs.

By studying the rocks and fossils of the Mesozoic era (the age of dinosaurs) here in Montana, my research group has discovered amazing specimens and learned incredible things about dinosaurs that people had never known before. We discovered the first dinosaur egg nests from the Western Hemisphere, the first evidence that dinosaurs cared for their young, the first dinosaur embryos, and evidence that dinosaurs traveled in gigantic herds. We also learned that dinosaurs grew very fast and lived short lives, that they were warm-blooded, and that birds evolved from them.

Understanding rocks and fossils allows people to use their imaginations to travel through time and view the development of Earth and the origin and evolution of life. In my opinion, geology is the most exciting branch of science on Earth!

Jack Horner

Professor Jack Horner, Curator of Paleontology, Museum of the Rockies, Montana, and consultant paleontologist for the *Jurassic Park* movies

Uluru, a giant sandstone rock formation in central Australia

CHAPTER 1

A world of rocks

We live on the surface of a giant ball of rock, Earth. The oldest rocks discovered so far on our planet are in northwestern Canada. They are around four billion years old. Other rocks are much more recent, and new rocks are forming all the time. Rocks develop in different ways—from hot, melted rock that has risen up from deep within Earth, from the fossil remains of animals and plants that solidify into rock over millions of years, and by the action of heat and pressure on ancient rocks inside Earth. But no rocks, however tough, last forever. They are worn away over time by water, wind, and other powerful forces of erosion. Earth's rocks are full of extremely valuable buried treasures. They give us precious stones, precious metals, and vital resources such as iron and coal.

Rock foundations

It may be hidden out of sight beneath buildings, plants, water, or ice, but rock covers the entire surface of Earth. There are three types of rocks on this planet, determined by how the rocks were formed—igneous, sedimentary, and metamorphic. These rocks are made up of solid chemicals called minerals. There are thousands of different minerals, including diamond, gold, and salt, but most rocks are made of a limited range. Pure sandstone, for example, consists only of the mineral quartz, the most abundant of all minerals. Granite is composed mainly of three minerals—quartz, feldspar, and mica.

▲ In this light micrograph of a slice of gabbro, an igneous rock, the mineral olivine appears as irregular-shaped crystals, and plagioclase feldspar minerals appear as long, slender crystals.

◄ The solar system, to which Earth belongs, began forming around 4.5 billion years ago, when an exploding star created a spinning cloud of gas and dust. The cloud condensed to make the young Sun and planets. Four rocky planets, including Earth, formed from dust closest to the Sun.

Where do rocks come from?

At the beginning of time, Earth was a giant, red-hot ball of molten matter—magma—that contained chemicals called elements. As the magma cooled down, its elements combined to form minerals. Around eight elements came together to make rock-forming minerals. Of these, oxygen and silicon are the two most common elements. They combine to form a group of minerals called silicates. A different combination of the elements produces a different rock-forming mineral.

Identifying minerals

Some minerals are not what they seem. Pyrite, for example, looks like gold to the untrained eye. Experts use a mineral's physical properties to identify it correctly. These include its color, habit (the typical appearance of the crystals, especially their shape and size), and hardness. A mineral's hardness is measured using Mohs' scale. This increases in hardness from 1 to 10. Diamond is the hardest mineral of all, so it has a rating of 10. Pyrite has a 6 to 6.5 rating, making it softer than diamond but a lot harder than gold, which ranges from 2.5 to 3. So, if you ever think you have struck gold—do not be fooled by the mineral's appearance and make sure that it has all the right properties.

Crystals

Crystals are the building blocks of most rocks. Often the crystals are too small to see, but in rare cases they can reach the size of a telephone pole. Crystals form when minerals crystallize, or solidify, into regular shapes with smooth, flat faces that meet in sharp edges. Each type of crystal has its own distinctive shape.

▶ These quartz crystals are pure, so they are colorless. Impurities give quartz a range of colors, including white, pink, yellow, blue, green, and brown.

▶ This is cleavelandite, a variety of the common mineral feldspar. It consists of thin plates of white crystals that can grow to almost one inch in diameter.

▶ During the early stages of Earth's formation, it was bombarded by meteorites and covered in volcanoes that spewed out lava. The oldest rocks on Earth are around four billion years old.

Changing Earth

Earth is like a giant egg. At its center is the "yolk," a metal ball called the core. The core is surrounded by dense rock called the mantle and an outer shell of hard rock known as the crust. The crust is broken into slabs called plates. The plates do not stay in the same place. They move, making Earth quake and volcanoes erupt and causing immense mountain ranges to form where plates collide.

▲ When plates move apart, a crack, called a rift, is created on the surface of Earth. This rift in Iceland has been caused by the separation of the North American and Eurasian plates, which are drifting apart at a rate of almost one inch every year.

▼ Earth's crust is broken up into a jigsaw puzzle of giant rock slabs called plates. The plates move in different directions (indicated by the arrows). Many of the planet's earthquakes and volcanic eruptions take place within the Ring of Fire, a belt that surrounds the Pacific Ocean where the Pacific plate meets a number of other plates.

Layered Earth

We live on the surface of the crust, so we know that it is solid rock. Scientific research tells us that the crust below the continents is thicker and less dense than the oceanic crust. The density of the next layer, the mantle, increases with depth. High temperatures and extreme pressures within this layer cause the rocks to flow like a thick, syrupy liquid. The core is divided into two distinct layers. The outer core is made out of iron, which is kept molten by temperatures of approximately 4,000°F (2,200°C). The inner core is a ball of iron and nickel. Although temperatures there reach around 8,130°F (4,500°C), the inner core is kept solid owing to extreme pressure.

▼ The Himalayas, the world's highest mountain range, formed around 50 million years ago when the island continent of India collided with the rest of Asia, buckling up the edge of the continental plates and parts of the oceanic crust between them.

Ring of Fire

NORTH AMERICAN PLATE

EURASIAN PLATE

Hawaiian hotspot

Ring of Fire

Ring of Fire

PACIFIC PLATE

PACIFIC PLATE

AFRICAN PLATE

Ring of Fire

SOUTH AMERICAN PLATE

NAZCA PLATE

INDO-AUSTRALIAN PLATE

Key
⎧ plate
  boundary
• active volcano
→ direction of plate movement

ANTARCTIC PLATE

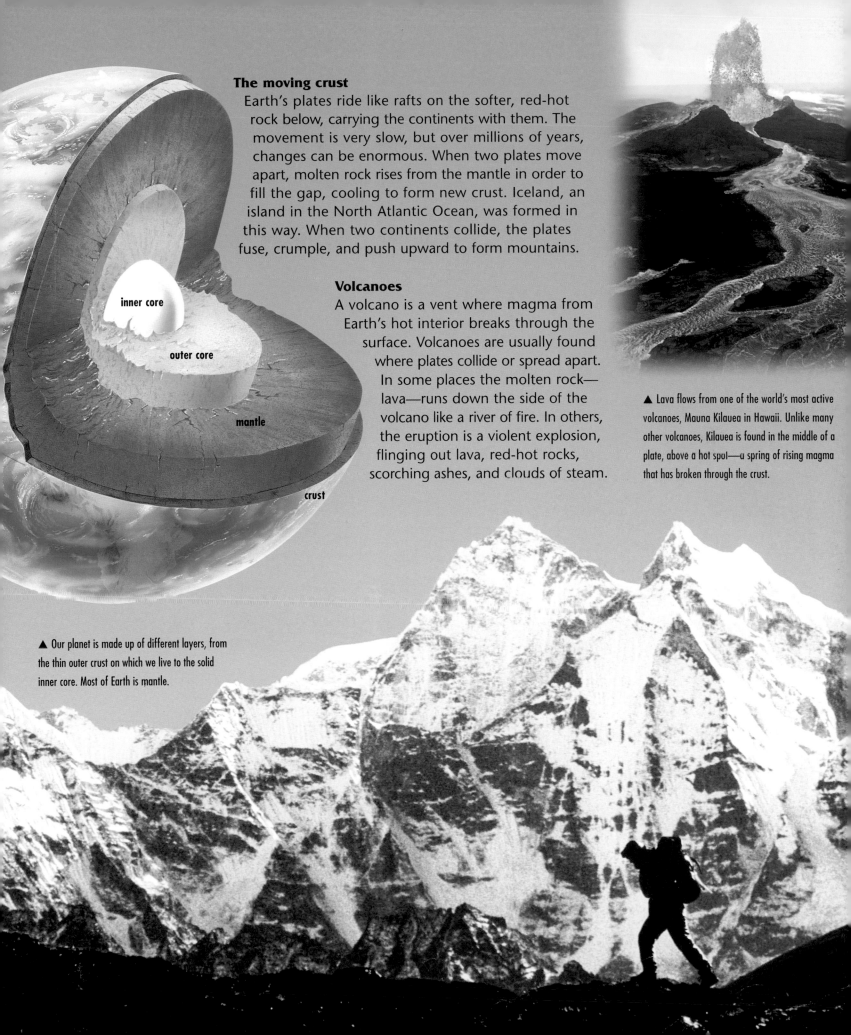

The moving crust

Earth's plates ride like rafts on the softer, red-hot rock below, carrying the continents with them. The movement is very slow, but over millions of years, changes can be enormous. When two plates move apart, molten rock rises from the mantle in order to fill the gap, cooling to form new crust. Iceland, an island in the North Atlantic Ocean, was formed in this way. When two continents collide, the plates fuse, crumple, and push upward to form mountains.

Volcanoes

A volcano is a vent where magma from Earth's hot interior breaks through the surface. Volcanoes are usually found where plates collide or spread apart. In some places the molten rock—lava—runs down the side of the volcano like a river of fire. In others, the eruption is a violent explosion, flinging out lava, red-hot rocks, scorching ashes, and clouds of steam.

inner core

outer core

mantle

crust

▲ Lava flows from one of the world's most active volcanoes, Mauna Kilauea in Hawaii. Unlike many other volcanoes, Kilauea is found in the middle of a plate, above a hot spot—a spring of rising magma that has broken through the crust.

▲ Our planet is made up of different layers, from the thin outer crust on which we live to the solid inner core. Most of Earth is mantle.

Rocks of fire

It is so hot deep within Earth's crust that some of the rock there is molten. When this molten rock cools down, it crystallizes to form solid rocks called igneous (fiery) rocks. Some igneous rocks, called intrusive rocks, form underground, where magma is forced into cracks or between rock layers and then solidifies. These rocks only appears at the surface millions of years later when overlying rocks have been eroded away. Igneous rocks that are formed when magma erupts from a volcano as lava and cools at the surface are called extrusive rocks.

▲ This is a light micrograph of a slice of granite. Granite is an intrusive igneous rock and consists mainly of grains of quartz, feldspar, and mica.

▼ The lava shown here flowing from Mauna Kilauea in Hawaii is called pahoehoe lava. As it cools, it develops a smooth surface under which molten lava continues to flow, giving it a wrinkled, ropelike apperance.

Igneous rock texture

The rate at which liquid rock cools determines the size and arrangement of the crystals inside the rock that is formed. Basalt, an extrusive rock, is formed when lava cools quickly. It is fine-grained because the crystallization process is rapid. Granite is an intrusive rock, formed when magma cools slowly underground. This means that the crystals have time to grow into coarse grains. Extremely fast cooling of magma, usually when it meets water, produces natural volcanic glass such as obsidian.

sill

dyke

batholith

◀ Magma escapes from belowground through vents in the crust. Underground, it may solidify to form dykes that cut across rock layers, or it may gather in reservoirs to form batholiths. Solid magma may also form sills. Sills run parallel to the rock layers.

Explosive rocks

If you shake a can of soda, pressure builds up inside the can. Once you open it, the pressure is released, and the liquid sprays out of the opening. Very violent volcanic eruptions occur in a similar way. The molten magma bubbles underground and is contained owing to pressure, until it breaks through the surface. The lava is expelled by force in the form of various-sized particles called pyroclastic rocks. But volcanoes do not only have destructive results. For example, volcanic ash produces very fertile soil that is ideal for agriculture.

Lava rocks

Lava can be compared to caramel. When it is hot, it is thin and runny, but as it cools, it becomes thick and sticky. Thick, sticky lava that contains large amounts of silicate minerals is called acid lava. This lava flows very slowly and forms steep-sided volcanoes. It often solidifies inside the volcano's vent, trapping gases inside. As pressure builds up, the volcano explodes, ejecting pyroclastic rocks. More fluid lava, called basic lava, forms flatter volcanoes or wells up through cracks in the sea floor.

▲ Basalt is the most common extrusive igneous rock found on Earth. When basaltic lava cools, it often forms hexagonal columns. This spectacular example is the Giant's Causeway in County Antrim, Northern Ireland. It consists of more than 40,000 columns and was formed around 60 million years ago.

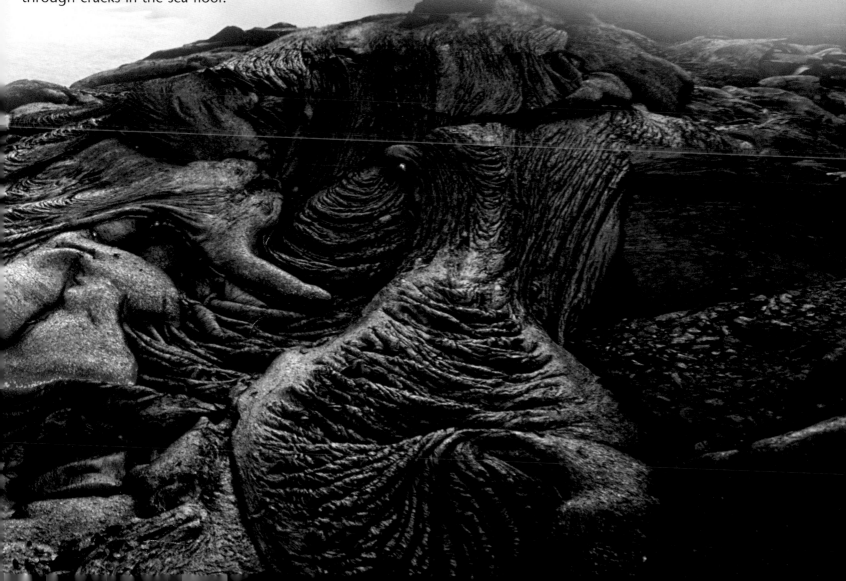

Layered rocks

Sand, mud, and even the remains of living organisms can all turn into rocks. These materials, known as sediments, settle on the floor of a river, lake, or sea, building up in layers called beds. These beds are later buried and compressed. Water, trickling through the sediment, deposits minerals that cement the sediments together to form sedimentary rocks. Millions of years later, when the rocks are exposed again, the layers are often visible as strata, or bands.

▲ The objects in this light micrograph of a slice of limestone are the fossilized remains of tiny shelled creatures called nummulites.

Secondhand rock

An exposed rock does not survive in one piece forever. Ice, wind, and water break it down into fragments, which are carried to low-lying areas such as valleys, lakes, or an ocean basin. Over time, the sediment grains, which range in size from microscopic particles to huge boulders, become compacted, forming rocks such as shale and sandstone.

Full of life

Earth's oceans are teeming with marine creatures. Many of them, such as corals and shellfish, have skeletons or shells made out of calcium carbonate. When these animals die, the soft parts decompose or are eaten by scavengers, while their skeletons sink to the sea floor, where they build up to form large beds of calcium carbonate. As more and more layers are added, the weight squeezes together and cements the layers at the bottom, eventually forming limestone. Sometimes the remains of the skeletons and shells are preserved in the limestone as fossils.

Limestone wonders

A secret world lies below the surface of regions formed from limestone. Caves wind through the rocks, opening out into huge chambers that are decorated with slender stone columns called stalagmites and stalactites. These natural wonders were formed over thousands of years by the action of rainwater, which turns calcium carbonate into calcium bicarbonate. This dissolves to create underground caves. Slow, repeated dripping from the cave ceilings has created hanging stalactites. Water that dripped to the ground created stalagmites, which grow upward.

▲ Water has hollowed out this enormous limestone cavern and has created clusters of hanging stalactites in the Cerrado savanna in Brazil. Stalactites and stalagmites are formed from tiny crystals of the mineral calcite. This is dissolved out of the limestone as water seeps through it. Sometimes a stalactite and stalagmite can meet in the middle to produce a formation called a pillar or column.

▼ Unobscured by vegetation, the sedimentary rock layers that form the Vermillion Cliffs in Arizona are very clearly visible.

Rocks that change

Heat, pressure, or a combination of both bake and squeeze rocks that are deep underground. These forces do not melt the rocks completely, but they can cause the minerals within the rocks to recrystallize and take on new forms. The result is a type of rock called metamorphic (changing) rock. The properties of a metamorphic rock depend on its parent rock—the original rock type—and the forces that formed it.

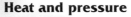
◀ ▲ Trinitite (left) is a metamorphic rock that formed during the test explosion of the world's first nuclear bomb in 1945 (above left). The extreme heat melted the sandy desert ground to create this glassy, greenish rock.

▼ Marble has been extracted from quarries, such as this one near Lucca in Italy, for centuries. A very attractive rock, it has been used as a material for sculptures, as a stone for the outside of buildings, and for pillars, colonnades, paneling, and floor tiles.

Baked rock
When you mix certain ingredients and bake them in an oven, the ingredients take on a new form such as a loaf of bread or a cake. Magma and lava "bake" the rocks that they come into contact with in a similar way, causing the minerals in the original rocks to change and a new metamorphic rock to be formed. The extent of the area affected by the heat of the magma or lava is determined by the molten rocks' temperature and volume. This rock-forming process is called contact metamorphism. It changes shale into hornfels and limestone into marble.

Heat and pressure
Many of Earth's great mountain ranges, including the Alps, Himalayas, and Andes, are made, in part, from metamorphic rocks. They were formed when continental plates collided, creating tremendous pressure and heat at the areas of contact. When plates collide and one is forced below the other, the submerged rocks are also metamorphosed by heat and pressure.

► These are the Atlas Mountains of northwest Africa. They contain metamorphic rock that began forming around 356 million years ago, when the African and American plates collided.

Transformation

Metamorphism over a large geographical area is known as regional metamorphism. This usually occurs underground, where temperatures are much hotter than aboveground and the pressure is greater because of the weight of the rocks above. Regional metamorphism can transform a sedimentary rock, such as shale, into a series of different rocks. Pressure turns shale into slate and slate into phyllite. Phyllite is transformed into schist through a combination of heat and pressure.

Crushed rock

As a great mass of rock grinds past another rock, the immense pressure at the areas where they meet crushes the rock at the meeting point, creating a metamorphic rock called mylonite. Although the structure of the new metamorphic rock differs from that of the parent rock, the minerals within the mylonite still contain the same chemicals. Mylonite forms less than two percent of all of the metamorphic rocks on Earth.

Rocks from space

Every day hundreds of small space rocks rain down on Earth and reach the ground as meteorites. Made out of iron, stone, or a mixture of both, meteorites are rocks that are left over from when the planets formed. As they rush through the sky, meteorites become extremely hot and can be seen as trails of light. These space rocks come in all sizes, from the very tiny, around one thousandth of a millimeter across, to the very large, often bigger than a house.

Meteorite hot spots

Most meteorites that fall to Earth are lost because they land among other rocks or in the ocean. The meteorites that have been recovered are often found in deserts, where the dry environment preserves them, and the lack of vegetation makes them more visible. More meteorites have been found in Antarctica than anywhere else. They remain frozen in the ice, some for up to one million years, and are carried with the ice as it moves. When the ice meets a barrier, it builds up. Winds scour the surface of the ice, and eventually the meteorites are revealed.

◄ Scientists from ANSMET (the Antarctic Search for Meteorite project) gather around a small meteorite. It is measured, photographed, and then placed inside a sterile bag for protection.

NORTH AMERICA

EUROPE

ASIA

AFRICA

SOUTH AMERICA

AUSTRALASIA

Key
● crater more than 6 mi. in diameter
● The Vredorft Impact Site

▲ This map show the location of all land meteorite craters of 6 mi. (10km) or greater in diameter. The ages of the impact craters range from around 1,000 years to two billion years. The Vredorft Impact Site in Free State Province, South Africa, is the largest known crater on land and measures 186 mi. (300km) wide. It was produced by a 6-mi. (10-km)-wide meteorite.

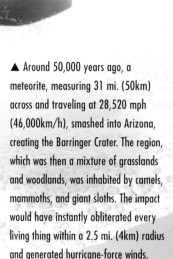

▲ Around 50,000 years ago, a meteorite, measuring 31 mi. (50km) across and traveling at 28,520 mph (46,000km/h), smashed into Arizona, creating the Barringer Crater. The region, which was then a mixture of grasslands and woodlands, was inhabited by camels, mammoths, and giant sloths. The impact would have instantly obliterated every living thing within a 2.5 mi. (4km) radius and generated hurricane-force winds.

Lunar and Martian rocks

Almost all of the meteorites that hit Earth come from the asteroid belt, which is the band of space rocks between Earth and Mars. However, scientists have identified around 20 meteorites as Moon rocks and around 12 as Martian rocks. The lunar rocks have a similar composition to samples brought to Earth by the *Apollo* and *Luna* missions. Gas trapped within some Martian meteorites matches the atmosphere of Mars, which was measured by the *Viking* probes that landed there in 1976.

▲ The Barringer Crater is around 1 mi. (1.6km) wide and 571 ft. (174m) deep, with a rim of boulders that rises 151 ft. (46m) above the level of the surrounding plain, which is now a desert. Most of the meteorite disintegrated on impact, although fragments have been found in the area.

▲ Rounded tektites, like this one, are called splash-form tektites. A second variety, called a Muong Nong tektite, has a blocky, fragmented shape.

Melted rocks

When large meteorites hit the ground, they explode. The intense heat from the explosion melts the surrounding rocks, forming small, glassy stones called tektites. Unlike meteorites, tektites are found only in certain, limited areas of Earth. This is because they dissolve slowly over time. The areas in which tektites are found are known as strewn fields, and these are located mostly in Australia, Java, the Philippines, and Indochina.

► Atlantic waves pummel cliffs on the south coast of Portugal, creating natural arches and columns called stacks.

Erosion

The surface of our planet is constantly changing. The movement of Earth's plates push up mountains and build up continents. Over time these new surfaces are worn back down again and are ground to dust in a process called erosion. Water, ice, and wind are the major causes of erosion. Bare rock is especially vulnerable because it is unprotected by soil and plants.

Coastal erosion

Wind moves over the ocean to produce pounding waves that erode the coast, undercutting cliffs, making them collapse, and leaving behind crumbling towers of rocks called stacks. Erosion occurs in two ways. Rocks and pebbles that are flung against a cliff face wear it away, or cracks in the rocks are enlarged as air compressed by incoming water expands when the water retreats. The rocks eroded from the coast are ground down by waves into shingle and sand, dragged along the sea floor, and eventually form beaches.

► Waves eat away at coastlines, causing them to retreat. Sometimes buildings are destroyed and sent crashing into the sea below—such as here, on the coast of Norfolk, England.

River erosion

Flowing water, loaded with stones and sand, is a powerful erosive force. Rivers erode hills and mountains and carry the debris down to the lowlands and the sea. A river's erosive power is the greatest in mountains, where its flow is at its fastest. The current is powerful enough to carry large boulders that bump along and scour the riverbed. Over millions of years large rivers carve out deep valleys.

Rivers of ice

Mountain ranges contain deep valleys that have been carved out by glaciers. A glacier is a slow-moving river of ice that flows downhill, carried forward by its enormous weight. As glaciers move, they pick up fragments of rock, which become frozen into the base of the ice. Any debris that falls on the surface works its way down to the bottom. As a result, the glacier acts like a sander, gouging deep into the ground and creating U-shaped valleys with steep sides and flat bottoms.

▲ Over the last million years the Colorado river has cut its way through layers of sedimentary rock, creating the Grand Canyon. The 277-mi. (446-km)-long gorge is up to 1 mi. (1.6km) deep and ranges in width from 3.7–18 mi. (6–29km).

◄ Strong winds, carrying sand and dust, blasted the soft volcanic rocks of Cappadocia, in Turkey, to create these strange formations. Many of them are inhabited by people.

Weathering

Most rocks and minerals are formed deep within Earth's crust, where temperatures and pressures differ greatly from the surface. But above the ground, they are vulnerable to attacks from the different chemical and physical processes that exist there. These processes are called weathering. The products of weathering are a major source of sediments for erosion and sedimentary rocks.

Raining acid

Some rocks are simply dissolved away by rainwater. Rainwater is naturally acidic. When it falls on chalk and limestone, the acid reacts with calcite in the rocks to form calcium carbonate, which dissolves in water. In towns and cities pollutants, such as sulfur, carbon, and nitrogen, combine with moisture in the air to form acids. When it rains or snows, these acids fall as acid rain, which is around ten times more acidic than normal rain. Statues are often worn away by this type of weathering.

▼ Rising like stone forests, the Guilin hills run alongside the Li river in China. Long-term weathering and water erosion have given these limestone features their peculiar shapes.

Freeze, thaw, and shatter

Ice can chisel its way through a rock, causing it to shatter. Water seeps into cracks in the rock, and then it freezes when the temperature drops. As it freezes, it expands and makes the crack bigger. When the ice thaws, even more water can penetrate the rock, expanding the crack further. A good place to see the weathering power of ice is on mountains. The endless cycle of freezing and thawing slowly turns the rock into piles of rubble called scree.

▶ This donkey train is walking a dangerous path through scree (loose stones and rocky debris) at the base of a mountain in Kings Canyon National Park in California. The animals and riders risk being hit by boulders tumbling down from higher ground, where weathering is causing rocks to break away from the mountain.

Plant power

A plant can be a powerful destructive force. Seeds that germinate in rock crevices expand as they draw in water. The force of the expansion can be strong enough to split a rock. Plant roots can work their way into cracks in soft rocks. As they grow and expand, they pry apart the crack, eventually splitting the rock.

▼ The roots of this tree are causing the rock to crack. Eventually, the rock will not be able to withstand the pressure and will break apart.

Raw materials

Rock is our most important natural resource. Everywhere you look there are objects made out of rock. For thousands of years slabs of solid rock, such as granite, slate, and sandstone, have been quarried and used in their natural state in order to construct buildings. Rocks are also processed to provide the minerals we need to make everything from roads and cars to silicon chips and jewelry.

▲ The Indian emperor Shah Jahan (1592–1666), who built the Taj Mahal as a tomb for his favorite wife, used many materials for its construction. These included Indian white marble and a range of precious stones such as agate from Yemen, coral from Arabia, garnet from central India, and onyx and amethyst from Persia. The building was begun in 1630 and took 23 years to complete.

◄ Formed from pebbles and cement, concrete is one of the most widely used building materials. Around 205,000 tons of concrete were used in the construction of the Millau Viaduct. This bridge connects the highway networks of France and Spain and spans almost 1.5 mi. (2.5km) across a spectacular gorge.

Recycled rocks

Building materials, such as bricks, cement, and concrete, are actually recycled rocks. Bricks are made from fine rock particles called clay. The clay is shaped into blocks when it is moist and is baked to harden it. Cement and plaster are made with minerals, including calcite and gypsum. These are heated to remove water and then are powdered. Once water is added to the minerals once again, they crystallize and solidify. When wet cement and pebbles are mixed together and the mixture hardens, solid concrete is formed.

▲ The trucks leaving this iron ore mine near Bahariya oasis in the Western Desert, in Egypt, are headed for smelting plants. There, their loads will be processed into iron. Iron is the fourth most common element In Earth's crust, and it is the most commonly used of all metals.

Stone tools

Around two million years ago, our early ancestors started creating and using basic axes. They were made from a type of quartz called flint. One million years later, hominids (early humans) with larger brains, known as *Homo erectus*, made a number of more sophisticated flint tools such as small blades and arrowheads for hunting. Today certain stones are used in many modern technologies. Rubies, for example, are used in lasers, while the powerful drills that dig through rocks in search of oil have hard diamond tips.

◄ More than 10,000 years ago, ancient flint workers shaped these flint arrowheads by hitting them against other stones. Each arrowhead was then tied to a wooden shaft so that it could be used for hunting.

Releasing metals

Since around 6,000 years ago, metals have played a key role in shaping human civilization, and the extraction and working of metals is still a vital industry in the modern world. Metals are mined from rocks, but only a few, including copper, gold, platinum, and silver, occur naturally in their pure state. Most metals are locked within mineral deposits called metal ores. Once the metal ores are mined, they must be crushed into smaller pieces and then treated with heat, chemicals, or a powerful electric current in order to separate the metal from its host material.

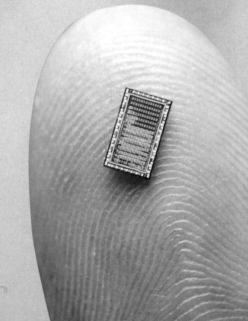

▶ Tiny silicon chips like this one function as a computer's electronic brain. A chip is a wafer-thin slice of silicon, an element that is found in Earth's crust. A single chip contains thousands of microscopic electronic parts.

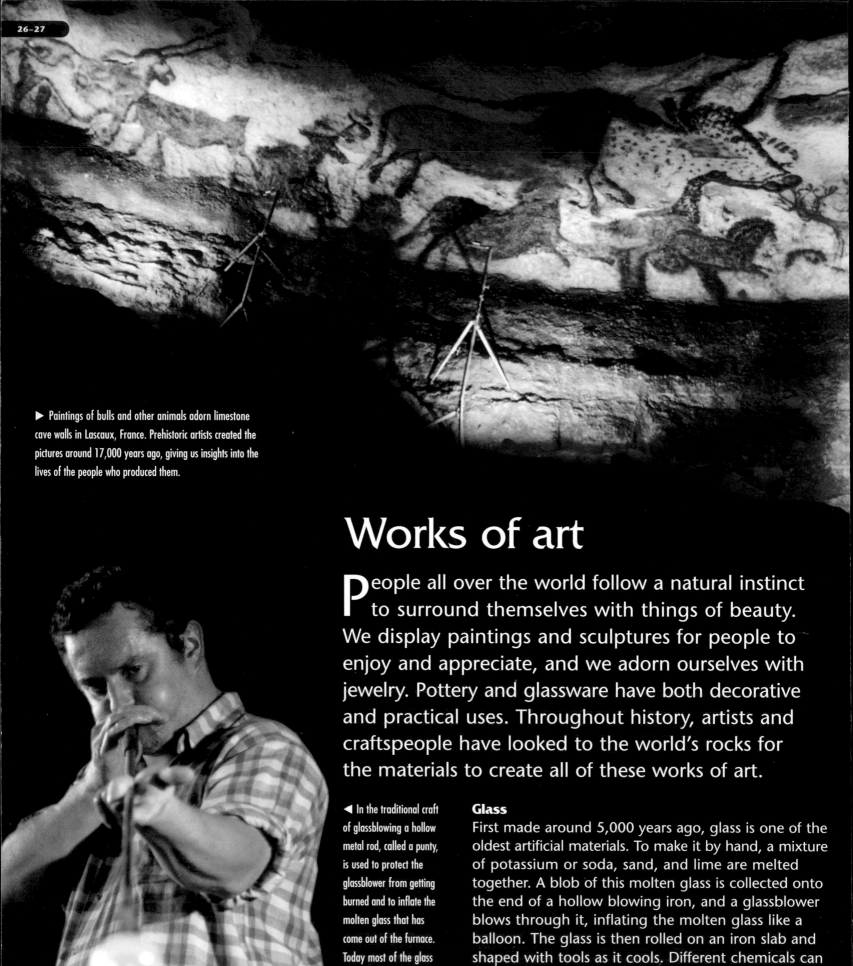

▶ Paintings of bulls and other animals adorn limestone cave walls in Lascaux, France. Prehistoric artists created the pictures around 17,000 years ago, giving us insights into the lives of the people who produced them.

Works of art

People all over the world follow a natural instinct to surround themselves with things of beauty. We display paintings and sculptures for people to enjoy and appreciate, and we adorn ourselves with jewelry. Pottery and glassware have both decorative and practical uses. Throughout history, artists and craftspeople have looked to the world's rocks for the materials to create all of these works of art.

◀ In the traditional craft of glassblowing a hollow metal rod, called a punty, is used to protect the glassblower from getting burned and to inflate the molten glass that has come out of the furnace. Today most of the glass we use is machine-made.

Glass

First made around 5,000 years ago, glass is one of the oldest artificial materials. To make it by hand, a mixture of potassium or soda, sand, and lime are melted together. A blob of this molten glass is collected onto the end of a hollow blowing iron, and a glassblower blows through it, inflating the molten glass like a balloon. The glass is then rolled on an iron slab and shaped with tools as it cools. Different chemicals can be added to make the glass colorful.

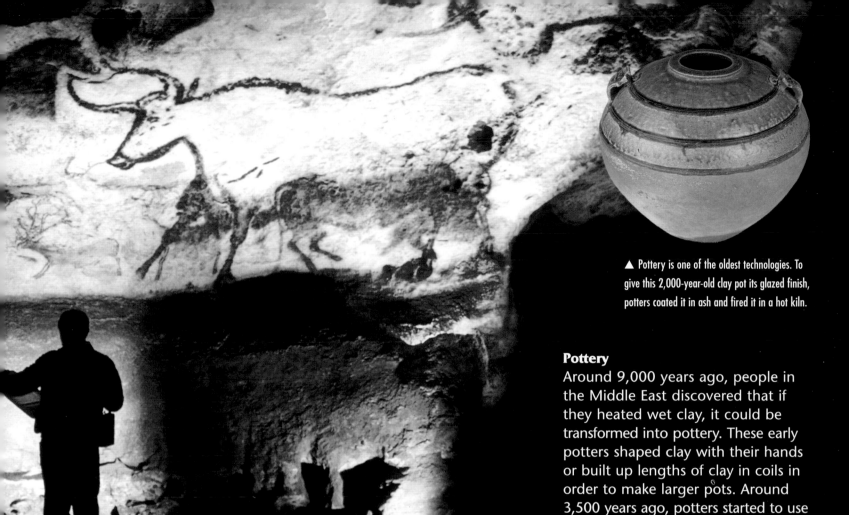

Pottery

Around 9,000 years ago, people in the Middle East discovered that if they heated wet clay, it could be transformed into pottery. These early potters shaped clay with their hands or built up lengths of clay in coils in order to make larger pots. Around 3,500 years ago, potters started to use small turntables, called wheels, to make their pots perfectly round. We know the history of pottery making because shards of pottery are the most common archaeological finds.

Cave art

The earliest artists, living around 40,000 years ago, painted animals on rocks or on the walls of the caves where they lived. Cave artists made paints by grinding minerals found in the earth into a powder and then mixing them with water. Red pigment was made from iron oxide or red ocher; white from kaolin or chalk; and black was either manganese dioxide or charcoal. The pigments were applied to the walls with clumps of fur or leaves or were blown through bone tubes.

Sculpture

By carving solid stone or pouring liquid metal into a mold, a sculptor can create a picture in three dimensions. Sculptors work with many types of stones, but marble is the most popular because it is a soft rock that carves easily. Sculptures cast from molds are usually made with bronze because of the unique way in which molten bronze becomes solid. After it is poured, it expands as it cools, filling every inch of the mold. When it solidifies, bronze shrinks, so it can be removed from the mold.

SUMMARY OF CHAPTER 1: A WORLD OF ROCKS

Where do rocks come from?

Scientists believe that Earth—and the solar system to which it belongs—began forming around 4.5 billion years ago from a cloud of dust and gas in space. Earth has three main layers —the crust, mantle, and core—but in the early part of its history the planet was a giant ball of magma. As the magma cooled, elements within it combined to form solid minerals, some of which formed rocks. Rocks are created in three different ways to produce igneous, sedimentary, and metamorphic types. These three groups are further subdivided into several types based on the rocks' physical attributes, including their texture and the chemicals and minerals they contain. Some of the rocks that are found on Earth do not actually come from this planet. They come from the asteroid belt, Mars, or the Moon

◄ This stone statue has become worn away by acid rain, caused by pollution in the atmosphere.

and fall to Earth as meteorites. Rock is our most important natural resource. It is used in its raw state, or it is processed for its minerals, which are used to make a range of items, from skyscrapers to bridges and from jewelry to computer chips.

A cycle of destruction and formation

The rock in Earth's crust is continually being weathered, eroded, and recycled. Rocks exposed on Earth's surface are worn down into sediments. These are carried away by glaciers, rivers, and the wind and are deposited in layers in lakes, deltas, dunes, and on the seabed, where, over millions of years, the sediments become compressed into sedimentary rocks. Molten rock within the crust solidifies to form intrusive igneous rocks. Intense heat and pressure deep underground change sedimentary and igneous rocks into metamorphic rocks. Movements in Earth's crust lift igneous and metamorphic rocks back to the surface, where they are broken down.

Go further . . .

Learn a lot more about rocks and minerals and how to start a collection at: www.rocksforkids.com

See a great comprehensive guide to minerals and gemstones at: www.minerals.net

Rocks and Minerals by Chris Pellant (Dorling Kindersley, 2000)

The Practical Geologist: The Introductory Guide to the Basics of Geology and to Collecting and Identifying Rocks by Dougal Dixon (Fireside, 1992)

Geologist
Studies the composition of Earth, its history, and the processes that affect it.

Geophysicist
Studies the physical properties of Earth, along with its internal composition, physical events such as earthquakes and volcanoes, and the planet's magnetic field.

Mineralogist
Investigates all aspects of minerals, including their origins, physical properties, chemical composition, and distribution in nature.

Volcanologist
Observes volcanoes, collects lava samples, and predicts eruptions.

Visit the Hall of Minerals and the Hall of Gems at the American Museum of Natural History:
Central Park West at 79th Street
New York, NY 10024-5192
Phone: (212) 769-5100
www.amnh.org

Discover how gold was mined underground during the last century:
Black Hills Mining Museum
323 West Main Street
Lead, SD 57754
Phone: (605) 584-1605
www.mining-museum.blackhills.com

Fossil dinosaur footprint

CHAPTER 2

Fossil remains

Fossils are the remains of plants and animals that were once alive. When they died, their remains were buried underneath sediments. The organisms gradually turned into fossils inside their protective tombs, and for millions of years they lay hidden from sight. Meanwhile, above the ground, Earth was undergoing dramatic changes—continents moved, seas expanded and disappeared, and mountains were formed and worn back down again. At the same time, new plant and animal species appeared and later became extinct. Some of these organisms were also fossilized, preserving valuable information about themselves and the conditions in which they lived. Today, when fossils resurface, paleontologists release them from the ground and begin unlocking their ancient secrets.

Body fossils

When an animal or plant dies, it is usually destroyed because a scavenging animal eats it or it rots away. Sometimes the animal's or plant's remains are buried before they can decay or be devoured, and if the conditions are just right, they are preserved as fossils. In very rare cases fossils of insects, bird feathers, and even dinosaur skin have been found. Usually only the hard parts of an organism, such as teeth, bones, and shells, become fossilized.

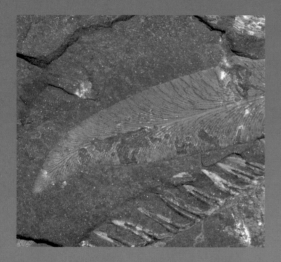

▲ Fossilized logs lie scattered across the ground in the Petrified Forest National Park in Arizona. Most are broken into segments, which are found in the correct order, suggesting that the logs fractured after they were buried and petrified.

▲ When leaves are compressed in beds of fine-grained sediments, their liquid and gaseous components are squeezed out. A film of carbon is sometimes left behind on the rock, preserving details of the leaf's shape in a process called carbonization.

A watery grave

Almost all fossils are preserved in sedimentary rocks formed from sediment such as clay, mud, and silt. These types of materials are laid down quickly in lakes, swamps, and oceans, providing ideal conditions for the rapid burial of a dead organism. This is one of the reasons why most fossils are the remains of animals that lived in or close to the water.

Mineral model

Rarely, the actual bone or shell of an animal may be preserved. Usually, however, the buried remains of an organism undergo considerable change. Water percolating through the rocks may dissolve the organic material and, at the same time, deposit a mineral in its place in a process called petrification. Once the process is complete, an almost perfect replica of the original structure is formed.

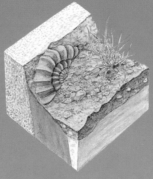

▲ Around 150 million years ago, a sea creature called an ammonite dies and falls to the seabed. Scavengers eat some of the animal's soft parts, and the rest rots away.

▲ Layers of sediment cover the empty shell, and they eventually harden into rock. Later movements of Earth's crust lift up these new rocks to form land above sea level.

▲ The forces of erosion wear down the rock, and the fossil eventually comes to light. A fossil hunter cracks open the stone to reveal the fossil and the mold it has left behind.

Petrified forest

Around 160 million years ago, a forest of pine trees in central Arizona died. Some of the trees were carried by streams or floods to a floodplain, where they were rapidly covered with mud and sand that was rich in silica. Groundwater later dissolved the silica and other minerals and deposited them in the cell tissues of the tree logs. This process continued very gradually until the logs were composed almost entirely of minerals and had become petrified.

Molds and casts

Sometimes a buried organism rots away completely or is dissolved by water and is not replaced. This may leave behind a cavity, called a mold, in the exact shape of the fossil. If the mold is later filled with minerals or sediment, it forms a lump in the shape of the original—called a cast. This type of fossil shows all of the external features of the object, just like Jell-O™ follows the shape of the mold that it is made in. However, a cast does not tell us anything about the organism's insides.

▲ They may look like flowers, but these fossils are actually sea creatures called crinoids, or feather stars or sea lilies. When they were alive, they attached themselves to the sea floor and used their featherlike feeding arms to filter microorganisms from the water. The earliest known crinoids date back to the early Ordovician period (around 510 million years ago).

◄ A fossil hunter holds an ammonite, one of the most common types of fossils. These marine animals emerged around 408 million years ago and died out around 65 million years ago during the mass extinction that also killed the dinosaurs.

Remarkable remains

On rare occasions fossils of soft tissues, which usually decay, are discovered. These finds are very exciting because they allow paleontologists to piece together a more complete picture of a creature for which they may already have fossilized hard parts. Under limited conditions, an entire animal may be preserved with both its hard and soft parts intact.

Preserved in peat

The extremely well-preserved remains of land animals and humans have been discovered in the cold, damp peat bogs of northern Europe. Peat is formed from mosses, sedges, and the woody parts of trees that have partially rotted in water. As the plants turn into peat, they release chemicals that destroy the bacteria that normally cause them to rot. Peat keeps out oxygen, which the bacteria need in order to survive, so once a bog organism is exposed to the air again, the natural process of decay begins.

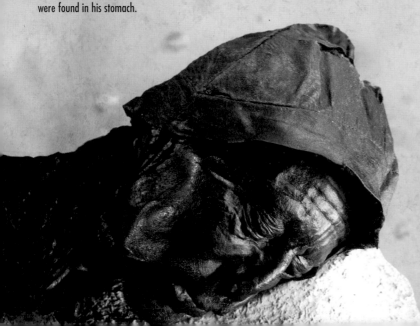

▼ In 1950 peat cutters in Tollund Fen, Denmark, unearthed the preserved body of a man who died in 100 B.C. His hat and belt were still in good condition, and the remains of his last meal, made from barley, were found in his stomach.

▲ Entombed in amber, this ancient mosquito has been preserved for millions of years with delicate parts of its body, such as its legs, antennae, and wings, still intact.

Jeweled insect

The most perfect fossils of all form when an insect becomes trapped in pine resin—the sticky fluid that oozes from a tree. The animal becomes completely immersed in the resin, which forms an airtight seal that prevents bacteria from attacking it, so it does not decay. The tree is subsequently buried and fossilized, during which time the resin changes into mineral amber, and the trapped creature is preserved whole.

The dinosaur with a heart

An animal's internal organs reveal how it functions physically. Unfortunately, internal organs are formed from soft tissues, so the chances of finding an organ as a fossil are rare. In 1997, however, the near-impossible happened when a fossilized *Thescelosaurus* dinosaur skeleton, containing the remains of its heart, was found near Buffalo in South Dakota. A CAT scan of the fossilized organ (similar to the type of scan used in hospitals to examine people) revealed that the dinosaur had a powerful, four-chambered heart that was more like a bird's or mammal's heart than the hearts of today's reptiles.

▲ The dark circle in the middle of *Thescelosaurus'* chest cavity is the dinosaur's fossilized heart. *Thescelosaurus*, a 13-ft. (4-m)-long, 663-lb. (300-kg) plant eater, lived 66 million years ago.

Deep freeze

During the last great ice age (around 100,000 to 10,000 years ago), a massive beast with long, shaggy hair and huge, curved tusks lumbered around what are now Africa, Eurasia, and North America. Called a mammoth, this animal was the ancestor of the modern-day elephant. We can be sure about its appearance because remarkably intact mammoth carcasses have been found in frozen ground in Siberia, preserved through refrigeration in a similar way to food stored in a freezer. The best-preserved mammoth found so far is a one year old known as Dima.

▶ Discovered in 2002 in northeast Siberia, Yukagir the mammoth is remarkably well preserved. Its long, curving tusks are almost undamaged, and a patch of fur can clearly be seen on its forehead.

Trace fossils

Life in the past has left not only its bodily remains but also its prints. They are the marks left behind as an animal went about its daily life, and these marks take the form of burrows, footprints, skin impressions, or even droppings. Fossils like these are called trace fossils. They are extremely useful to paleontologists because they provide valuable insights into how an animal lived and behaved.

◀ This is fossilized dung. Experts believe that it came from a turtle that lived during the Miocene epoch (23.3 to 5.2 million years ago).

▼ To produce this picture, an artist's impression of a traveling herd of apatosaurs was merged with a photograph of paleontologists examining a trail of apatosaur footprints on the Colorado Plateau. Smaller footprints are found on top of those made by the adult dinosaurs, which tells us that the young walked at the rear of the herd.

◀ *Maiasauras* nests were simply holes scraped out of the ground. They were up to 6.5 ft. (2m) in diameter and contained around 25 eggs, which were around the size of a grapefruit. The hatchlings were around 12 in. (300mm) long.

Nesting behavior

More than 40 dinosaur nests have been found scattered across an area covering 2.5 acres in Montana. The nests belong to *Maiasauras*, dinosaurs that lived during the late Cretaceous period (see pages 50–51). We know that these dinosaurs settled in a large group during the breeding season. Several nests were within easy reach of one adult. This suggests that the adults shared the responsibility of nurturing and protecting the young.

Making tracks

Ancient animals often left footprints in soft mud, and sometimes the mud baked hard before the print disappeared. If the print was later filled with sediment, the footprints were sometimes preserved as fossils. A track of footprints can indicate where the animal went, whether it traveled as part of a group, and even if it dragged its tail.

You are what you eat

It may seem like an unpleasant job for many people, but some paleontologists specialize in examining fossilized animal droppings. Called coprolites, they can provide important clues about the diet of the animal that dropped them. For example, a coprolite may contain the bones of other animals, suggesting that the animal was a carnivore.

▲ Holding a rock hammer and a sample bag is British paleontologist and geologist Mary Anning (1799–1847). In the 1820s Anning found the first complete skeleton of a *Plesiosaurus* and a fossil of the first-known flying reptile, *Dimorphodon*.

Early paleontology

We understand what fossils are thanks to dedicated work that began around 300 years ago. Before then, people had some strange ideas about fossils. From around A.D. 450 until the 1600s, European Christians believed that fossils were planted by the devil or that they were the remains of animals that perished in the biblical flood. In China fossil bones and teeth were believed to be dragon bones and were collected and used as medicine. Greek philosophers who lived between 610 B.C. and 425 B.C. held beliefs closer to what we know to be true. Because they found fossils of marine creatures in rocks above sea level, they proposed that this land once lay under the sea.

▲ Mary Anning discovered many of her finds, including *Dimorphodon*, in the fossil-rich cliffs of Dorset, England. This flying reptile from the Jurassic period probably soared from the cliffs, snatching fish from the sea with its wide, toothed jaws.

▲ Fossilized great white shark teeth, which resembled this one, were once known as tongue stones. In ancient times the Roman author Pliny the Elder suggested that they fell from the sky or Moon. Later peoples thought that they were the tongues of serpents that Saint Peter had turned to stone. Niels Stensen identified them correctly in 1666.

▲ This print shows Baron Georges Cuvier lecturing about paleontology in Paris, France. Cuvier was the first person to prove that extinctions of past life-forms have taken place. He believed that migrating animals sometimes repopulated areas that had been wiped out.

Making the link

In 1666, while studying the teeth of a shark, Danish scientist Niels Stensen (1638–1686) was struck by their resemblance to stony objects, called *glossopetrae*, or tongue stones, found in certain rocks in Italy. For centuries people had held various ideas about what these stones were. Stensen noticed that there were differences between tongue stones and the teeth of today's sharks, concluding that they came from sharks that no longer existed. As tongue stones were found on land, he correctly suggested that the ocean once covered the land, allowing sharks to live there.

Catastrophe theory

At the beginning of the 1800s French geologist and naturalist Baron Georges Cuvier (1769–1832) proposed that catastrophes, such as sudden land upheavals and floods, had wiped out entire species. This explained, he said, the sudden changes in the types of animal remains contained within the different levels of strata. Cuvier's catastrophe theory remained popular until Swiss naturalist Louis Agassiz (1807–1873) put forward an alternative theory in 1837. He suggested that certain young rocks, believed to be flood deposits, were actually deposited by glaciers during a great ice age. Initially, other scientists rejected the idea, but they were eventually persuaded, and Agassiz's theory is still accepted today.

◄ The man featured in the book is Sir Richard Owen (1804–1892), the English zoologist who coined the word "dinosaur" in 1841. Sitting on the books are *Megalosaurus* and *Iguanodon* fossil teeth, which were found in the 1820s, and a *Scelidosaurus* foot and limb, first described in 1861.

Relative ages

William Smith (1769–1839) worked in a coal mine and later surveyed canal routes in England in the late 1700s. During this time, he made detailed studies of local rocks and the fossils he found in them. He observed that each layer in a section of sedimentary rock had characteristic fossils that did not show up in other layers, and the fossil-bearing layers followed a consistent sequence that could be predicted. Smith found this order of appearance in other rock sections across the country and concluded that rocks containing the same fossil species were the same age. Using his theory, today's geologists match strata of the same age in different geographic areas.

Fossil fuels

Most of the energy used today on our planet comes from burning fossil fuels, including coal, petroleum, and natural gas. Fossil fuels are also used to produce synthetic materials such as plastic and nylon. These fuels were formed, over millions of years, from the remains of plants and animals, so once we extract them, they cannot be replaced.

▲ Mine shafts are dug down to seams, or layers, of coal below the surface. Miners then dig a network of tunnels, cutting the coal from the seams with drills and computer-controlled cutting machines.

▼ The dense swamps of the Carboniferous period featured a variety of plants, including horsetails, lycopods, and ferns. These reached heights of up to 66 ft. (20m). Today we see the fossilized remains of these carboniferous plants in the form of coal.

From plant to coal
When we burn coal, we release energy that has been trapped for almost 300 million years. Originally, this energy was captured by swamp-dwelling plants during photosynthesis (the process by which plants use sunlight in order to convert carbon dioxide and water into food). After they died, the plants decomposed, undergoing different stages of change. In the early stages bacteria decayed the plants, forming peat, a soft, fibrous, brown-black substance. The peat was then buried and compressed under the weight of more sediment and rotting plants. Gradually, it once again changed to produce lignite and then bituminous coal, and, finally, if temperatures and pressures were high enough, anthracite coal.

From plankton to crude oil and gas

Microscopic plants and animals, called plankton, live near the surface of the sea. When they die, they sink to the seabed, where they are buried in clay and mud. Over millions of years, these sediments turn into rocks, which are covered with more layers. As the layers on top of the remains build up, the pressure and temperature also increase. This process gradually converts the organic matter into crude oil and gas, which float up through pores and fractures in the rocks. Eventually, the oil and gas meet a layer of rock, known as a cap rock, that traps them in the sedimentary rock below. There, they form a reservoir.

Refining oil

When crude oil is heated, substances within it called hydrocarbons (compounds that are made of only hydrogen and carbon atoms) turn into different gases. Each gas condenses back into a liquid at a different temperature, and in this way oil can be separated into different fractions, or parts. The separating process, called fractional distillation, takes place in a fractional column. As well as fuel for cars and aircraft, crude oil is separated into lubricating oils, bitumen (tar) for making roads, and chemicals known as petrochemicals. These are used to make various products, including plastics, textiles, fertilizers, detergents, and paints.

▲ Oil platforms house workers and the machinery needed to drill for and extract oil and gas in the ocean. The platforms float on the sea or, like this one, sit on legs that stand on the seabed.

▶ Given the right conditions, this living plankton, found off the coast of Scotland, could be turned into oil over the next 150 million years. The crude oil we use today is made from plankton that lived during the Jurassic period.

SUMMARY OF CHAPTER 2: FOSSIL REMAINS

Fossilization

Fossils are the preserved remains of plants or animals that lived millions of years ago. Certain conditions are needed in order for fossilization to occur. The organism must have had hard parts that are capable of being fossilized. Once the organism has died, it must be buried rapidly by sediment. This slows down decomposition and prevents scavengers from eating or removing the remains. The sediment must remain undisturbed as it solidifies into rock, and then the remains become a fossil. Most fossils are animals and plants that lived in or close to water, where the conditions for preservation are usually much better than on land. Most of the land animals and plants that have been fossilized were preserved in sediments, either because they drowned or fell into the water, or they were swept into the water by floods or other unexpected events.

A fossilized ammonite, a type of shellfish that lived in the Jurassic period

Modes of preservation

Fossils are found in different forms. On rare occasions the actual skeleton is preserved, and under very unusual circumstances an entire animal may be preserved. More often, however, the skeletons and shells are mineralized. This occurs when water trickling through the rocks gradually dissolves the original material and deposits minerals in its place. Sometimes the remains are dissolved completely or they rot away, leaving a hole in the exact shape of the organism, called a mold. If the mold fills up with rock minerals, it becomes a cast fossil. Many plant fossils, which show the actual shapes of the leaves and stems, are made of carbon. Footprints, made in soft mud, can become preserved under layers of sand or silt. Fossilized prints provide clues to an animal's behavior.

Go further . . .

 See how fossils are formed and how and where they are collected at:
www.rom.on.ca/quiz/fossil

Find out how to start your own fossil collection at:
http://web.ukonline.co.uk/conker/fossils

Learn more about fossil fuels, where they come from, and their many different uses at:
www.energyquest.ca.gov

Atlas of the Prehistoric World by Douglas Palmer (Random House, 1999)

Fossils: The Key to the Past by Richard Fortey (Smithsonian Books, 2002)

 Naturalist
Studies plants and animals and the way they evolve.

Paleomagnetist
Investigates fossil magnetization in rocks and sediments in order to record the spreading of the sea floor and changes in Earth's magnetic field over millions of years.

Paleontologist
Studies the fossil remains of ancient plants and animals in order to trace the evolution of life and Earth's geological history.

Petroleum geologist
Explores for oil and gas by studying and mapping below the seabed or under the surface of the land.

 Visit one of the world's finest collections of fossils at:
Smithsonian National Museum of Natural History
10th Street and Constitution Ave. NW
Washington, D.C. 20560
Phone: (202) 633-1000
www.mnh.si.edu

Find out about the U.S. oil industry at:
California Oil Museum
1001 E. Main Street
Santa Paula, CA
Phone: (805) 933-0076
www.oilmuseum.net

Paleontologists searching for fossils on a rock face in Madagascar

CHAPTER 3

Records in rocks

To a geologist, rocks are like the pages of a history book—they tell the story of Earth. The rock layers are much more difficult to read than the pages of an ordinary book because they are often fractured, folded, or upside-down. Some of the layers are scattered over a wide area, while others are missing altogether. The key to the layers and their order lies in the fossils contained within them. The fossils also reveal a lot about the history of Earth and the life living on it. Scientists first realized that Earth's seas and land continually move across the face of the planet when fossils found on mountains were identified as marine creatures. Supported by geological evidence, the geographic distribution of certain fossils proves that the continents were joined together and drifted apart at different times in Earth's history. The fossil record also shows us that life evolved from simpler forms and that mass extinctions have occurred in the past.

Reading rocks

The rocks that you see around you are filled with many clues about the past. Paleontologists and geologists work like detectives, scrutinizing each layer of rock to reveal the conditions under which they were formed. The composition of the rock, its structure, and the fossils that it contains provide the vital information with which we can build a detailed picture of a particular environment's history.

▶ By looking at local sites and comparing them with rock formations in different locations, geologists and paleontologists have pieced together a lot of the history of Earth and its life-forms.

Local history

If a sequence of rocks has been undisturbed, the layers at the bottom are older than those at the top. The beds of rock then represent periods of time that follow on from one another. If you find a thick layer of limestone, packed full of fossil shells, and it has a layer of red sandstone on top, you can assume that the area was once covered by water, and later it was a desert environment.

Comparing dates

A rock layer formed from clay in one location looks very different from an exposed layer of limestone in a different place, but they may include the same collection of fossil species. If the species were short-lived in geological terms, then it is certain that the two sediments were laid down within that same narrow period of time. When geologists compare rock strata from location to location, they pay particular attention to the fossils contained within the strata.

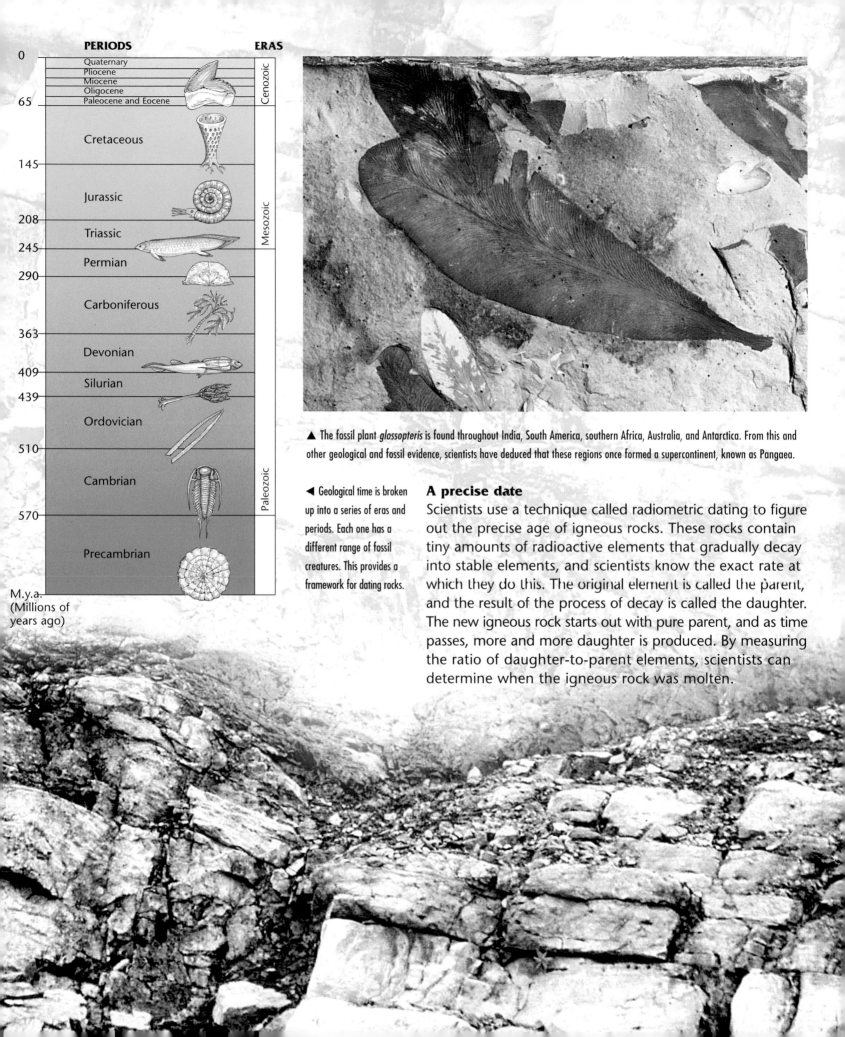

PERIODS	ERAS
Quaternary	Cenozoic
Pliocene	
Miocene	
Oligocene	
Paleocene and Eocene	
Cretaceous	Mesozoic
Jurassic	
Triassic	
Permian	
Carboniferous	
Devonian	Paleozoic
Silurian	
Ordovician	
Cambrian	
Precambrian	

0
65
145
208
245
290
363
409
439
510
570

M.y.a.
(Millions of
years ago)

▲ The fossil plant *glossopteris* is found throughout India, South America, southern Africa, Australia, and Antarctica. From this and other geological and fossil evidence, scientists have deduced that these regions once formed a supercontinent, known as Pangaea.

◀ Geological time is broken up into a series of eras and periods. Each one has a different range of fossil creatures. This provides a framework for dating rocks.

A precise date

Scientists use a technique called radiometric dating to figure out the precise age of igneous rocks. These rocks contain tiny amounts of radioactive elements that gradually decay into stable elements, and scientists know the exact rate at which they do this. The original element is called the parent, and the result of the process of decay is called the daughter. The new igneous rock starts out with pure parent, and as time passes, more and more daughter is produced. By measuring the ratio of daughter-to-parent elements, scientists can determine when the igneous rock was molten.

Early life

▲ Cyanobacteria are one of the earliest known forms of life. These organisms are still found today in Australia, where they form colonies in distinctive mounds called stromatolites.

In southwest Greenland volcanic rock that is almost four billion years old lies on top of sedimentary rock. Within this deeper, older layer are carbon traces of the earliest known living organisms. The oldest actual fossils date back 3.5 billion years. Discovered in Western Australia, they consist of chains of microscopic single-celled organisms that look like blue-green algae. It took a further 2.5 billion years before multicelled animals appeared on the planet.

▼ *Marella splendens*, a primitive arthropod, was the most abundant of the Burgess Shale animals.

Soft bodies

The oldest animal fossils appear in rocks from the Late Precambrian period (610 to 570 million years ago), which contain a variety of soft-bodied marine organisms. Originally, most of the fossils were believed to represent types of anemones and jellyfish. However, one fossil, called *Kimberella*, has recently been interpreted as an ancestor to the mollusks (animals such as snails and shellfish), while another, known as *Spriggina*, may be an ancestor of the arthropods, which include today's insects, spiders, and crustaceans. Many of the others, including *Hallucigenia sparsa*, *Opabinia regalis*, and *Wiwaxia corrugata*, are unlike any creatures that are alive today.

▶ *Amiskwia sagittiformis* does not belong to any known animal group. It had a head with two tentacles, a trunk with stumpy side fins, and a flattened tail.

Cambrian explosion

Between 533 and 525 million years ago, during the Cambrian period, marine animals diversified rapidly. More than 100 major animal groups appeared, especially those with hard shells. Only around 30 of the groups survived to this day. The fossils that tell the story of this event, which is often called the Cambrian explosion, were found in a fossil bed called Burgess Shale in the Canadian Rockies. There, soft-bodied and hard-bodied animals were buried in an underwater mud slide and preserved in water that was so deep and starved of oxygen that they did not rot away.

Life at sea

When the Ordovician period began around 510 million years ago, the area north of the tropics was almost completely water. Most of the land was collected into the supercontinent Gondwanaland, which was shifting toward the South Pole. Earth's climate was mild, and there were many warm seas. On the seabed were crustaceans called trilobites and hinged-shelled invertebrates called brachiopods. There were also reef-building animals such as corals and sea lilies. Swimming above them were squidlike cephalopods and some early fish. When Gondwanaland finally settled on the South Pole during the Late Ordovician, the climate changed, and huge glaciers formed, draining shallow seas. Around 60 percent of all marine invertebrates disappeared from the fossil record at this time.

◄ The rocks found in a deposit of shale, called the Burgess Shale, in Canada, contain large numbers of Cambrian fossils. Many of the fossils include the soft parts of organisms.

◄ *Hallucigenia sparsa* had protective spines on its back and clawed tentacles on its underside.

◄ ► *Wiwaxia corrugata* (left), an animal that is not related to any other known creature, had long, protective spines on its back. *Opabinia regalis* (right) was a soft-shelled predator with five eyes. It used grasping spines at the end of its long snout to catch its prey.

▲ Called *Isotelus gigas*, this species of trilobite lived during the Ordovician period. Its streamlined shape helped it plow through sediment on the seabed as it searched for food, while its body armor protected it from predators. An adult *Isotelus gigas* reached almost 16 in. (40cm) in length.

The age of fish

Following the ice age of the Late Ordovician period, the climate warmed up in the Silurian period, causing large ice formations to melt. This led to a major rise in sea levels, creating new marine habitats. Coral reefs formed over vast areas, and fish increased in variety and quantity. This continued into the Devonian, when two main lines of fish appeared in the seas—the sharklike fish, with their soft, cartilaginous (gristly) skeletons, and the bony fish.

▲ This is the fossil remains of *Bothriolepis*. Fossils of this species have been found throughout the world. These fish had a set of lungs, so they could survive out of water for short periods of time. They lived mainly in freshwater and fed on algae from the bottom of lakes.

Jaws

Fossils of ostracoderms, the earliest known vertebrates, appear in the Ordovician and Devonian strata of North America and Europe. Most of them were heavily armored with bony plates and scales, especially in the head. These fish had mouths, but they were unable to bite or chew since they had no jaws. They probably fed by sucking up mud and other debris and filtering it through their gills in order to extract food. The first jawed fish, the placoderms, appeared in the Silurian (439 to 408 million years ago). Like the ostracoderms, these fish were partly covered with bony armor.

▶ This is *Osteolepis macrolepidotus*, a mid-Devonian fossil fish from the Orkney Islands in Scotland. It belongs to an extinct group of freshwater fish called the rhipidistians. Many scientists believe that amphibians evolved from this group.

Flurry of fish

The Devonian period, which began around 409 million years ago, is often called the Age of the Fish. Many of the jawless fish were still living at this time, and the placoderms were plentiful. By the end of the Devonian period, there were two distinct evolutionary lines of bony fish. The first of these, the ray-finned fish, diversified dramatically over time, and this group contains the majority of the fish alive today. The other, the lobe-finned fish, are represented today by only six species of lungfish and the coelacanth, although there were many more species in the Devonian period. These could breathe air, just as the modern lungfish can, and they could probably move around on their lobed fins. Scientists believe that the earliest land vertebrates evolved from this group.

▲ Coelacanths flourished in the Mesozoic era (245 to 65 million years ago). Up until 1938, when a coelacanth was caught off of South Africa, scientists believed that this ancient species was extinct. Local fishermen, however, knew of its existence long before then.

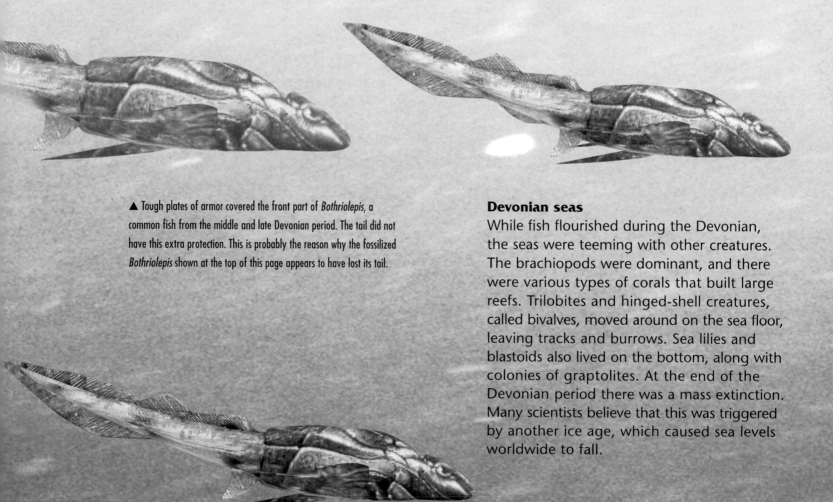

▲ Tough plates of armor covered the front part of *Bothriolepis*, a common fish from the middle and late Devonian period. The tail did not have this extra protection. This is probably the reason why the fossilized *Bothriolepis* shown at the top of this page appears to have lost its tail.

Devonian seas

While fish flourished during the Devonian, the seas were teeming with other creatures. The brachiopods were dominant, and there were various types of corals that built large reefs. Trilobites and hinged-shell creatures, called bivalves, moved around on the sea floor, leaving tracks and burrows. Sea lilies and blastoids also lived on the bottom, along with colonies of graptolites. At the end of the Devonian period there was a mass extinction. Many scientists believe that this was triggered by another ice age, which caused sea levels worldwide to fall.

Life moves on land

For millions of years, life existed only in the oceans. Then, around 450 million years ago, mossy plants began growing near water. Around 420 million years ago, arthropods (a group that includes today's insects, spiders, and crustaceans) emerged from the water and fed on the land plants. During the Devonian period, amphibians came ashore to spend part of their lives on land. Reptiles evolved from amphibians in the middle of the Carboniferous period and became the first completely land-dwelling vertebrates, or animals with backbones.

▼ *Eryops* was an amphibian that lived around 250 million years ago. Its jaws were full of sharp teeth, indicating that this crocodilelike creature was a carnivore.

▲ This is a model of a trigonotarbid, one of the earliest known land dwellers and a relative of the modern-day spider. Trigonotarbid fossils, dating back more than 400 million years, have been discovered by paleontologists in the Ludlow Bone Bed in Shropshire, England.

Arthropods on land

Arthropods were highly adapted to life out of the water. By the time they appeared on land, they had already evolved light bodies and spindly but strong legs that worked against the force of gravity. Their hard outer shells retained moisture. In the Silurian period centipedes, millipedes, and trigonotarbids became the first arthropods to move onto land. The fossil record shows that these arthropods were joined by nonflying insects and spiders in the Devonian period and land scorpions and flying insects in the Carboniferous period.

▶ This fossil dragonfly, called *Urogomphus eximus*, is around 140 million years old and was recovered from a fossil-rich site in Solenhofen, Germany. Dragonflies first took to the skies around 330 million years ago.

Fish out of water

Around 375 million years ago, amphibians became the first four-legged animals to move onto land and breathe air. The earliest, such as *Ichthyostega*, closely resembled the lobe-finned fish, which had already used their fleshy fins to shuffle ashore. Later amphibians, however, were much better equipped for moving around on land. In most cases they had well-defined limbs and feet for walking, a rib cage to support their body, and a strong neck that enabled them to keep their heads off the ground. Like today's amphibians, they still returned to the water to mate and lay eggs.

Complete adaptation to life on land

The reptiles were the first vertebrates to make a complete adjustment to terrestrial life. They had two major advantages over their amphibian ancestors—scaly, waterproof skin that provided protection and prevented them from drying out and the ability to lay their eggs on land. The early reptiles were meat eaters, but during the Permian period many different species evolved, including plant eaters. Some even returned to the water. One group evolved into turtles, and another produced the snakes and lizards. Mammals evolved from yet another group of reptiles.

▲ Pterosaurs were flying reptiles that fed mostly on fish. Fossils reveal that they had slim, hollow bones and wings made out of skin that stretched between their long finger bones and legs. They could glide for long distances on rising air currents. An occasional flap of their wings provided extra power to stay up in the air.

Ruling reptiles

Reptiles dominated Earth during the Mesozoic era between 245 and 65 million years ago. Many would have been very familiar to us today. There were large turtles and tortoises, crocodiles, and many lizards and snakes. In addition to these creatures, there were groups of reptiles that have now completely vanished. These were the land-based dinosaurs, the winged pterosaurs, and families of reptiles that returned to the seas from which their ancestors had come.

► Fossils of *Therizinosaurus* have been found in the Gobi desert in Mongolia. This dinosaur roamed coniferous forests there around 75 million years ago, using its 27-in. (70-cm)-long claws to pull tree branches toward its mouth in order to feed on the leaves.

Dinosaurs
There were many different species of dinosaurs, and they came in all sizes. The early dinosaurs were all carnivores, and they walked on their hind legs. Plant-eating types developed later, and some of them returned to walking on all four legs. Some also reached enormous sizes. For example, *Seismosaurus* was more than 130 ft. (40m) long—the length of four buses. Other plant-eating dinosaurs, such as *Triceratops,* had bony armor or horns to use as a defense against predators. The meat eater *Velociraptor* was only 6.5 ft. (2m) long but hunted prey in packs and could kill much bigger animals.

Up in the air and below the waves

While the dinosaurs were busy populating the land, pterosaurs conquered the air, and the seas were the domain of marine reptiles. The largest pterosaurs had wingspans of up to 40 ft. (12m), although most were not much bigger than modern-day pigeons. The marine reptiles include mosasaurs, which were up to 33 ft. (10m) long; plesiosaurs, which measured up to 43 ft. (13m) in length; and ichthyosaurs, which resembled dolphins. Although these reptiles spent their lives in the water, they all breathed air and were therefore forced to surface in order to fill their lungs before disappearing back into their underwater world.

▶ *Archaeopteryx* had a number of reptilian features, such as claws and a long tail, but it is believed to be one of the earliest birds. The shape of its feathers meant that it could probably glide. Other fossil finds suggest that dinosaurs first evolved feathers in order to stay warm before birds used them to fly.

▲ Sue, the largest and most complete *Tyrannosaurus rex*, was found in South Dakota. It is now on display at the Field Museum of Natural History in Chicago, Illinois. Although *T. rex* had between 50 and 60 bone-crunching teeth, this dinosaur was not a ferocious killer. Instead, it was a scavenger, feeding on the remains of dead creatures.

Decline of the reptiles

All of the dinosaur families living in the late Cretaceous period died out around 65 million years ago, as did many other species. Their disappearance has been linked to an enormous meteor strike, which left a vast 112-mi. (180-km) -wide crater in the Gulf of Mexico. Scientists believe that the gas and dust from this impact filled the atmosphere, blotting out the Sun for hundreds of years. This theory is supported by evidence in the geological record. Traces of the chemical element iridium are found in sediments deposited at the immediate end of the Cretaceous period. Iridium is rare on the planet's surface but occurs in high concentrations deep underground and in meteorites that fall to Earth.

Prehistoric plants

Around 450 million years ago, plants began their invasion of the land. Like animals, plants evolved special adaptations for their terrestrial life. Many developed veinlike structures, called vacuoles, that carry water and nutrients, gathered up by the roots, to the upper parts of the plant. Some developed woody stems so that they could grow taller, and all plants evolved efficient methods of reproduction that were adapted to their surroundings.

▲ *Pecopteris* was one of the most common plants in the coal-forming swamps of the Carboniferous period. Many examples of this fern have been preserved as fossils.

Spores and seeds

A group of primitive plants, called psilophytes, were the first plants to appear on land. The earliest forms had no leaves. Soon after the psilophytes appeared a group of plants called microphyllophytes, with small leaves, emerged. Both of these plant groups reproduced using cells called spores, and they needed moist conditions to complete their life cycle. Halfway through the Carboniferous period there were large forests of woody plants. Among them were horsetails, cone-bearing cordaitales, and seed ferns. The seed ferns produced seeds instead of spores. The ability to reproduce by seeds allowed these plants to survive in much drier habitats.

▼ Male pinecones of modern-day *Pinus sylvestris* release a cloud of pollen into the air. The pollen is blown by the wind and can reach trees that are some distance away. The ability to do this allowed pine trees to colonize and then dominate the land in the Mesozoic era.

▼ As shown in this artist's impression, the early Devonian land was treeless, and most of the plants were no taller than 15 in. (40cm). The leafless plants in the front section of this picture are a type of psilophyte.

The rise of the conifers

During the Mesozoic era (245 to 65 million years ago), conifers, which are similar to modern-day giant redwoods, and tall cycads dominated the forests. These plants belong to a group called gymnosperms and were well adapted for colonizing the land. Gymnosperms produce pollen, usually inside male cones. The pollen floats on the wind to the female cone, where it fertilizes the ovules (eggs). The seed that results can survive a drought in a dormant state in the female cone, waiting for a favorable season to begin its growth. Most of the finds of petrified wood are gymnosperms such as *Araucarioxylon*, a tree that flourished throughout the Mesozoic era.

▶ *Ginkgo biloba*, which is often called the maidenhair tree, is a prehistoric species that still survives today. In the wild it is now restricted to a small region in China, but around 200 million years ago it grew all over the world. The maidenhair's earliest known leaf fossils date back 270 million years.

▶ Modern-day magnolias, like this one, have pollen grains that are similar to fossil pollen dating from the early Cretaceous period. The earliest flower-bearing plants probably evolved from seed ferns. Today there are more than 200,000 species of angiosperms.

Flowering plants

Flowering plants first appeared more than 125 million years ago. Flowers allowed the plants to form partnerships with bees, butterflies, and other flower-feeding insects. While the animals fed on nectar within the flowers, they also carried pollen from flower to flower. These plants, called angiosperms, also provided a protective covering for the seed in the form of a burr or a fruit. The earliest known flowering plant is *Archaefructus sinensis*, which was found in the Liaoning province in China. Although the fossil has no petals, there are closed fruits with the seeds inside.

Mammals

Mammals first appeared during the Triassic period (245 to 208 million years ago), when reptiles still dominated the land. For a long time they remained small and unobtrusive, probably adopting a nocturnal lifestyle. No one knows for sure why, but mammals did not become extinct along with the dinosaurs at the end of the Cretaceous period. Once the dinosaurs were gone, mammals, like the dinosaurs before them, adapted to diverse habitats and developed a large range of shapes and sizes, spreading across almost every part of the globe.

▼ The 10-ft. (3-m)-long, 3-ft. (1-m)-tall giant rodent *Phoberomys pattersoni* weighed as much as a buffalo. This guinea-piglike creature lived in wetlands during the Miocene period, around eight million years ago. Today rodents make up more than 40 percent of all mammal species.

Mammallike reptiles

After the reptiles evolved from the amphibians, one group, called the synapsids, took a radically different path to the other reptiles, evolving mammallike features. Among the most advanced of these reptiles were the cynodonts, which first appeared in the early Permian. Almost-complete fossils of *Thrinaxodon*, an early Triassic cynodont species that lived between 240 and 245 million years ago, have been found in South Africa. This creature's skeleton had adapted to give it a more upright stance and gait. Unlike reptiles, its jawbones were adapted for chewing. Small holes in the bone of its snout suggest that it had whiskers. This implies that *Thrinaxodon* also had fur and was therefore warm-blooded, unlike reptiles.

Early mammals

By the late Cretaceous, the three main groups of mammals had emerged. These were the placentals, which carry their young inside themselves until the babies are fully developed; marsupials, which give birth to underdeveloped young that are then carried in the mother's pouch; and egg-laying mammals, called monotremes. The first known placental mammal was *Eomaia scansoria*, a tiny shrewlike species that lived 125 million years ago. *Steropodon galmani* is the earliest known monotreme species, dating back 100 million years. *Pariadens kirklandi*, the first marsupial for which we have fossil evidence, lived around 95 million years ago.

▲ The duck-billed platypus, which is native to eastern Australia, is one of only two modern-day monotremes. Its skeleton has a number of reptile features, and, like reptiles, it lays eggs. The platypus spends most of its time in the water and breeds in burrows dug into a riverbank.

Mammals of Australia

When the dinosaurs began colonizing the planet, all of the continents were joined together in one landmass. In contrast, when mammals, especially the placentals, began dominating Earth from 65 million years ago, the continents were already separated. Although not closely related, similar-looking animals evolved independently on different continents, filling the same types of habitats. In Australia, which became separated from the rest of the continents before the placental animals became the dominant group, the marsupials diversified. These included the now extinct, 6.9-ft. (2.1-m)-long rhinoceroslike *Diprotodon*, as well as the marsupial lion *Thylacoleo*.

▼ *Hyaenodon horridus* was a carnivorous mammal that lived through the Oligocene, around 35 to 23 million years ago. Their skulls reached around 11 in. (28cm) long, and their jaws were lined with large teeth that were adapted for biting and crushing prey.

Humans

We belong to a group of mammals called the primates, and our closest living relatives are apes. By four million years ago, the human evolutionary line, called hominids, had become distinct from other primates. The hominids are divided into two groups—*Australopithecus* and *Homo*. They were all bipedal (two-footed, upright walkers), and up until around two million years ago, they lived only in eastern and southern Africa. *Homo erectus* was the first hominid to leave Africa, moving to Asia and later Europe. Eventually, *Homo erectus* evolved into *Homo sapiens*—modern-day humans.

▲ Experts believe that *Homo erectus* and early *Homo sapiens* used this hand ax for a range of tasks, from carving wood to butchering animals. It was found, along with other axes, in the Olduvai Gorge in Tanzania, Africa.

Brain boxes

Around four million years ago, our early ancestors had a small brain of around 21 in.^{3} (350cm^3), and they walked on their knuckles. *Australopithecus*, which walked partially upright, emerged four to three million years ago, with a 27 in.^{3} (450cm^3) brain. By 1.5 million years ago, *Homo erectus* had a brain size of between 52–67 in.^{3} (850–1,100cm^3) and a completely upright posture. This hominid was a skillful toolmaker and was probably able to speak. Our own species, *Homo sapiens*, emerged around 100,000 years ago with a brain size of around 85 in.^{3} (1,400cm^3)—the size of a large grapefruit.

▶ This is a model of a male *Australopithecus afarensis*, our earliest known hominid ancestor. The most famous *Australopithecus afarensis* is a young female nicknamed Lucy, whose 3.2-million-year-old remains were found in 1974 in Hadar, Ethiopia.

▲ These skulls belong to some of our early ancestors and relatives—*Australopithecus africanus* (**1**); *Homo habilis* (**2**); *Homo erectus* (**3**); *Homo sapiens sapiens* (**4**); and Cro-Magnon human (**5**). *Homo habilis*, which had a significantly larger brain than *Australopithecus africanus*, was the first known toolmaker.

Walking tall

Around 3.6 million years ago, a volcano erupted in Laetoli in Tanzania, spewing hot lava across the land. Many creatures walked through the cooling lava, including three *Australopithecus* individuals—two adults and a child. These hominids left a trail of footprints in the soft rock, which hardened and were later buried beneath sediment and ash. A team led by Mary Leakey (1913–1996) found the path in 1976. The discovery showed that a primate species walked on two feet at least 3.6 million years ago. This tied in with evidence from fossil *Australopithecus* bones.

▲ Mary Leakey and her team carefully brush away loose sediments during a dig in Tanzania in 1977. Over the course of this expedition, the team discovered the fossil remains of 25 early hominids and 15 new animal species, as well as the fossilized footprints of three *Australopithecus afarensis*.

Getting a grip

Australopithecus had shorter, less flexible thumbs and narrower fingers—relatively speaking—than ours. They could exert a lot of force in a powerful grip, probably using rocks and sticks for tasks such as cracking nuts. From around three million years ago until around 1.5 million years ago, the thumbs of hominids became longer and more maneuverable and the fingertips broadened, giving them a more flexible grip. This allowed hominids to make and use tools, which became more complex over time.

▶ Studies of the tracks in Laetoli have revealed that they were made by *Australopithecus afarensis*, which walked from heel to toe as we do. We have also learned that this hominid's feet had a well-developed arch, very similar to ours.

SUMMARY OF CHAPTER 3: RECORDS IN ROCKS

Hard evidence

Earth has undergone many changes in its 4.6-billion-year history. These changes have been recorded in rock strata that were laid down over millions of years. Fossil remains found in these rocks also provide information about the conditions in which animals lived. For more than 100 years, geologists have used the geological record to produce a time line for Earth's history, which they divide into eras and periods.

Fossil *Archaeopteryx* found near Workerszell, Germany, in 1951

The story of life

The first known life-forms—bacteria and algae—did not appear until around 3.5 billion years ago, and the oldest known multicelled animal fossils are found in rocks that are between 610 and 570 million years old. Between 533 and 525 million years ago, animal life diversified rapidly. Jawless fish emerged around 510 million years ago, sharing the seas with trilobites, corals, and sea lilies. Mossy plants became the first organisms to live on land around 450 million years ago, and around 420 million years ago, some arthropods began feeding on these land plants. Amphibians emerged from the water around 45 million years later. Reptiles evolved from the amphibians, becoming the most dominant creatures on Earth during the Mesozoic era (254 to 65 million years ago). During this time, some reptilian groups developed into dinosaurs, pterosaurs, and marine reptiles. Mammals, which first appeared in the Triassic (245–208 million years ago), became prominent after the dinosaurs became extinct 65 million years ago. Emerging around four million years ago, our earliest ancestors evolved fairly recently in the history of life on Earth.

Go further . . .

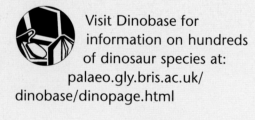

Visit Dinobase for information on hundreds of dinosaur species at: palaeo.gly.bris.ac.uk/dinobase/dinopage.html

View an illustrated guide to mass extinctions of the past at: www.bbc.co.uk/education/darwin/exfiles/index.htm

Trace the story of evolution at: www.pbs.org/wgbh/evolution

From the Beginning by Katie Edwards and Brian Rosen (The Natural History Museum, 2000)

The Complete World of Human Evolution by Chris Stringer and Peter Andrews (Thames & Hudson, 2005)

Anthropologist
Explores the origins of humans, along with their behavior and their physical, social, and cultural development.

Evolutionary biologist
Investigates the origin and ancestry of species, as well as the way that they evolve over time.

Micropaleontologist
Investigates fossils of ancient single-celled organisms that are found in rocks and sediments.

Paleoecologist
Studies the relationship between fossil species and the environments in which they lived.

Visit Sue, the most complete *T. rex* found to date: The Field Museum 1400 S. Lake Shore Drive Chicago, IL 60605-2496 Phone: (312) 922-9410 www.fieldmuseum.org

Discover how evolution has shaped the history of life on Earth at: Australian Museum, 6 College Street, Sydney, NSW 2010, Australia Phone: +612 9320 6000 www.amonline.net.au

Meet our hominid ancestors at the Life Galleries: Natural History Museum, Cromwell Road, London SW7 5BD, U.K. Phone: +44 (0)20 7942 5000 www.nhm.ac.uk/visit-us/galleries

Glossary

amber
The fossilized resin of trees, usually honey-yellow or various shades of red. Often small animals, such as insects, have been preserved in amber.

ammonite
An extinct group of marine mollusks with coiled shells. Their closest living relative is probably the modern nautilus.

anthracite
A hard form of coal with a very high carbon content.

atom
A tiny part of an element, such as carbon or oxygen, from which all materials are made.

batholith
A large mass of igneous rock, with a surface area of more than 36 sq. mi. (100km^2) and a typical depth of 19 mi. (30km) that forms when magma cools deep inside Earth's crust.

bituminous
Describes a soft coal with a high carbon content.

calcium carbonate
A chemical compound of calcium and oxygen. Limestone is mostly made from calcium carbonate.

carbon
An element that is one of the building blocks of life. Pure carbon comes in several forms, including graphite, which is a hard, grayish-black rock. Coal is also rich in carbon.

carbonization
A type of fossilization in which liquids and gases are pressed out of a living organism, leaving behind a thin film of carbon. Plants are often fossilized in this way.

crust
The outermost layer of Earth. The crust lies over the mantle.

Slate cliffs, North Pembrokeshire, Wales

crystal
A substance in which the molecules are arranged in a regular repeating pattern.

deposit
To lay down sediments such as sand, mud, or gravel in a new place.

dinosaur
A member of a group of reptiles that lived from around 230 million years ago up until around 65 million years ago.

diversified
Became more varied or different. When animals or plants diversify, new forms develop.

element
Any substance that cannot be broken down into simpler substances.

erosion
The wearing away and removal of rocks and exposed land by water, wind, and ice.

extinct
Describes a species of living organism that has died out and disappeared. Dinosaurs, for example, are extinct.

Fossil ammonite

extrusive igneous rock
Igneous rock that forms on Earth's surface from lava.

fossil
The remains, traces, or impressions of once-living organisms that have been preserved.

glacier
A mass of ice that forms on land and flows slowly downhill under its own weight.

igneous rock
A type of rock that forms when magma or lava cools and hardens.

intrusive igneous rock
Igneous rock that forms underground when magma cools slowly.

lava
Molten rock that is forced out of a volcano during an eruption.

light micrograph
A photograph taken using a light microscope.

magma
Molten rock that is deep underground in Earth's mantle or crust.

mammal
A warm-blooded animal with fur or hair and a backbone. Mammals breathe air and feed their young on mother's milk.

mantle
The layer of Earth between the outer core and the crust.

Amethyst crystals

metamorphic rock
A type of rock that forms when other rocks are subjected to heat, pressure, or both.

meteorite
A rock from space that reaches the surface of a planet without burning up in the planet's atmosphere.

microscopic
Something that is so small that it is invisible to the naked eye and can only be seen with a microscope.

mineral
A substance with a crystalline structure that occurs naturally. Rocks are made up of minerals.

mineralized
When a substance is replaced with minerals or has minerals added to it, it is mineralized.

Mohs' scale
A scale used to measure the relative hardness of minerals.

molecule
The simplest unit of a chemical substance, made up of two or more atoms.

radioactive
Giving off radiation or rays of energy generated by the disintegration of atoms.

radiometric dating
A technique for dating igneous rocks that involves measuring the proportions of radioactive elements and stable elements within the rocks.

reef
A ridge or low island of limestone, usually found in the shallow parts of tropical oceans. Reefs are formed from the skeletons of corals and other marine creatures.

rock
A solid mixture of minerals. Rocks are divided into three main groups—igneous, sedimentary, and metamorphic.

scree
Loose rubble and gravel on a mountain slope, caused by weathering.

sediment
Material that sinks to the bottom of a lake or sea or material that is deposited by wind, water, or glaciers.

sedimentary rock
A type of rock, such as sandstone or limestone, that forms when sediment is squeezed together and cemented over long periods of time.

slate
A metamorphic rock that has a fine grain and a sheetlike appearance.

solar system
The Sun and all of the bodies orbiting around it, including the planets, their satellites, asteroids, and comets.

molten
The hot, liquid state of a solid substance that has been melted by heat.

ore
A rock from which a valuable mineral is mined.

peat
A dark-brown organic material produced by the breakdown of plants that grow in marshes and wetlands.

period
A division of geological time.

petrification
A process that replaces living materials, such as wood or bone, with minerals.

plate
A large slab of Earth's crust; also known as a tectonic plate.

primate
Any member of the group of animals that includes humans, apes, monkeys, and lemurs.

pyroclastic rock
Rock made from fragments blown out of a volcano during an explosion.

Ant trapped in resin

stalactite
An iciclelike mineral formation that hangs from the ceiling of a cave.

stalagmite
A pillar of minerals that stands up from the bottom of a cave.

strata
Layers of sedimentary rock.

tektite
A glassy rock that may be formed by the impact of a large meteorite.

vertebrate
An animal with a backbone, or spine.

volcano
A vent in Earth's crust through which molten rock, hot gases, and ashes escape.

weathering
The breaking down of rocks by various processes such as freezing and thawing.

Index

Acknowledgments

The publisher would like to thank the following for permission to reproduce their material. Every care has been taken to trace copyright holders. However, if there have been unintentional omissions or failure to trace copyright holders, we apologize and will, if informed, endeavor to make corrections in any future edition.

Key: *b* = bottom, *c* = center, *l* = left, *r* = right, *t* = top

Cover *l* Ardea Francois Goher; Cover *c* Corbis/Layne Kennedy; Cover *r* Corbis and page 1 Corbis/Layne Kennedy; 2–3 Getty Images; 4–5 Frank Lane Picture Agency (FLPA)/Gerry Ellis; 7 Getty Taxi; 8–9 Science Photo Library (SPL)/Mark Garlick; 8*cl* SPL/Mark Garlick; 8*tr* SPL/Dirk Wiersma; 9*tr* SPL/Geoff Tompkinson; 9*cr* SPL/Charles D. Winters; 10–11 Getty Stone; 10*tl* SPL/Daniel Sambraus; 12–13 Getty Imagebank; 12*tl* Corbis/Lester V Bergman; 13*tr* Getty/Photonica; 14–15 Getty/Taxi; 14*tl* SPL/Alfred Pasieka; 15*tr* FLPA/Claus Meyer; 16–17 Zefa; 16*tl* SPL/U.S. Army; 16*cl* SPL/David Parker; 16*bl* Zefa; 18*cr* Antarctic Search for Meteorites Program/Nancy Cabot; 19*tr* Corbis/James L. Amos; 19*cl* SPL/Ray Simons; 20 FLPA/Roger Tidman; 20–21 Corbis/Bryn Colton; 20*tr* Getty Imagebank; 21*tl* Corbis/Tom Bean; 21*cr* Photolibrary.com; 22–23 Corbis/Dallas and John Heaton; 23*tr* Corbis/Galen Rowell; 23*br* Corbis/Lefkowitz; 24–25 Corbis/Chuck Savage; 24*tl* Getty/Stone; 25*tr* Getty Imagebank; 25*cr* SPL/George Roos, Peter Arnold Inc.; 25*br* Corbis/Roger Du Buisson; 26–27 Getty/NGS; 26*bl* Corbis/Adam Woolfitt; 27*tr* Corbis/Honeychurch Antiques; 27*br* Getty Robert Harding Picture Library; 28 SPL/Adam Hart-Davis; 29 FLPA Roger Tidman; 30–31 SPL Martin Bond; 30*tl* SPL/Dirk Wiersma; 30*cl* Photolibary.com; 31*tr* Corbis/Layne Kennedy; 32 SPL/Sinclair Stammers; 32*bl* Corbis/Werner Forman Archive; 33*tr* SPL/Jim Page, North Carolina Museum of Natural Sciences; 33*br* Corbis/Francis Latreille; 34*b* Corbis/Louie Psihoyos; 34*tl* SPL/Sinclair Stammers; 35*tl* Natural History Museum, London; 36 SPL/Michael Marten; 36*b* SPL; 37*tc* SPL/Sinclair Stammers; 37*tr* Mary Evans Picture Library; 37*bl* SPL/John Reader; 38–39 Open University/John Watson ; 38*tl* Corbis/James L. Amos; 39*tr* Zefa; 39*cr* Corbis/Craig Aurness; 40 Corbis/Layne Kennedy; 41 Getty NGS; 42–43 Corbis; 43*tr* SPL/Martin Land; 44*cl* SPL/John Reader; 44*tr* SPL/Alan Sirulnikoff; 45*br* Corbis/Kevin Schafer; 46*cl* Corbis James L. Amos; 46–47 SPL/Christian Darkin; 47*tl* SPL/Sinclair Stammers 47*tr* SPL/Peter Scoones; 48*tl* Jason Dunlop; 49*tr* Natural History Museum, London; 49*br* SPL/Alexis Rosenfeld; 51*tr* Corbis/Sally A. Morgan; 51*cr* Corbis/Philip Gould; 52–53 John Watson Open University; 52*tl* Corbis Kevin Schafer; 52*bl* SPL/Claude Nuridsany & Marie Perennou; 52*tr* SPL/Malcolm Warrington; 52*br* Corbis/Peter Smithers; 54–55 SPL/Christian Darkin; 55*tr* FLPA/Foto Natura Stock; 55*cr* Corbis/Dorling Kindersley; 56*tl* SPL/John Reader; 56*tl* SPL/Pascal Goetgheluck; 56–57 SPL/Javier Trueba, MSF; 57*tr* John Reader; 57*br* John Reader; 58 Corbis/Sally A. Morgan 59 FLPA/Ken Day; 60*bl* Corbis/Layne Kennedy; 60–61*t* FLPA/Maurice Nimmo; 61*tr* FLPA/Mark Moffett; 64 Getty Photonica

The publisher would like to thank the following illustrators:
Sebastien Quigley 20–21; Steve Weston 18–19, 34–35, 36–37, 44–45, 48–49, 50–51; Peter Winfield 10*bl*, 18*bl*